ARCHIMEDES
THE MAN WHO INVENTED THE DEATH RAY

Shoo Rayner

Published by Shoo Rayner

www.shoorayner.com

ISBN 978-1-908944-351

A CIP catalogue record for this book is available from the British Library.

Rome - 200 BC

What did you do in the Punic Wars, Daddy?
I won the battle of Syracuse and gained the Island of Sicily for the Roman Empire, son.
You're so brave and clever, Daddy.

Marcus Claudius Marcellus closed his eyes and remembered the greatest battle of his life.

"The siege of Syracuse dragged on for two years," Marcus explained.

We didn't just fight the people who lived in that city, we fought the cleverest man that ever lived - Archimedes - the man who invented the Death Ray!
Wowee! Tell me about him, Daddy. Tell me about the man who invented the Death Ray!

Archimedes Invented the Lever

Archimedes invented things that we use every day. Sometimes he would get his ideas in unusual places.

Ah! This see-saw gives me a great idea.

A lever is a solid beam or rod made from something strong like wood or metal.

The lever is balanced on a hinge, which is called a fulcrum. It looks just like a see-saw.

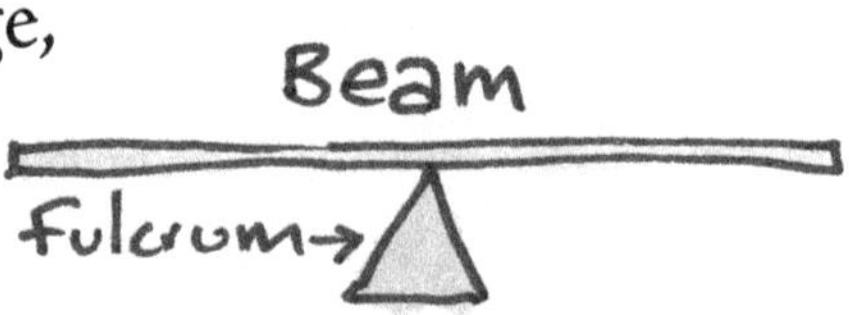
Beam
Fulcrum

Hey!

When a heavy person sits on a see-saw, the lighter person gets stuck up in the air.

That's better!

To balance a light person and a heavy person the fulcrum must be moved nearer to the heavier person.

With the fulcrum placed at one end of a lever, a small amount of weight on the longer side of the lever will lift a heavier weight on the shorter side.

100

The fulcrum can be tall, which makes it very useful for moving heavy things. It's like a simple crane.

Archimedes said:

"Give me a lever long enough and I will move the world!"

ARCHIMEDES INVENTED PULLEYS

All that lifting stuff got Archimedes thinking.

Rope is good for
lifting things. I wonder
if I can make a lever
with that too?

Archimedes realised that the ropes and the bar, which make a simple, lever crane, are really just the same as a piece of rope thrown over a bar on top of some poles.

But now the fulcrum is in the middle so the weight is too heavy to lift.

So Archimedes invented the pulley.

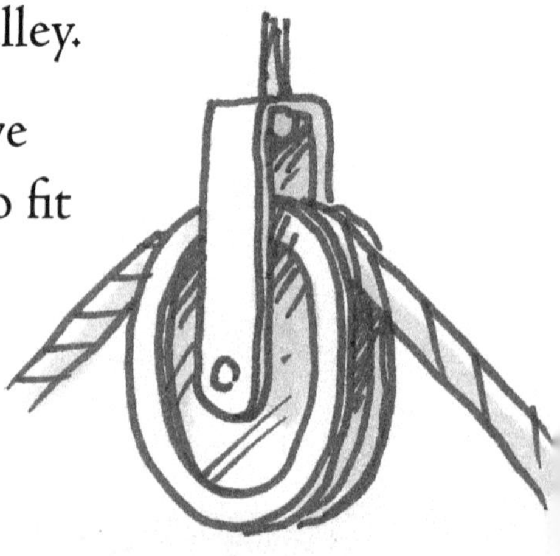

A pulley is a wheel with a groove on the outside rim for the rope to fit in. The pulley lets the rope move easily around the axel that goes through the hole in the middle of the pulley wheel.

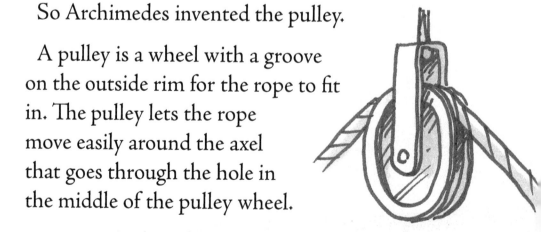

One pulley wheel is exactly like a pair of scales. To balance each side, equal weights must be attached.

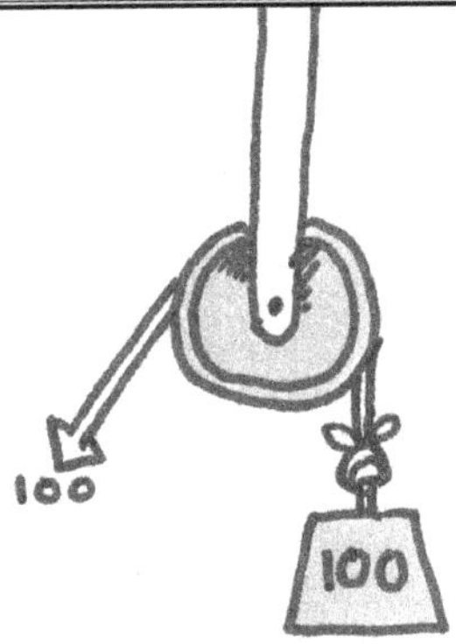
100
100

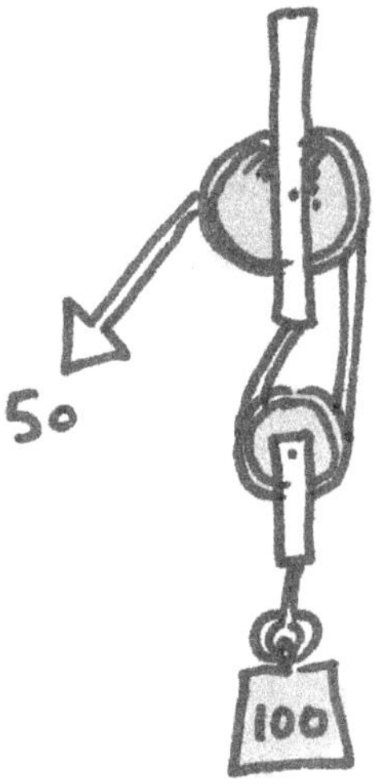
50
100

Adding another pulley is like moving the fulcrum. An extra pulley means that the heavy weight can be balanced with half its weight. That means it becomes half as heavy to lift.

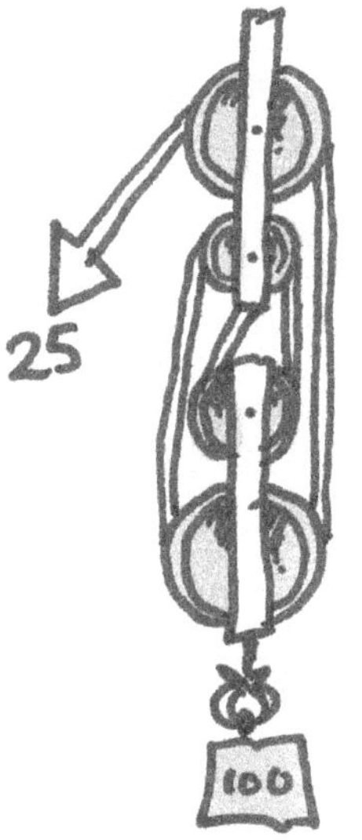
25
100

Four pulleys make the weight even easier to lift. Now the weight is balanced by a quarter of its weight, so it is four times less heavy to lift.

You still do the same amount of work with a pulley. You just have to pull the rope twice or four times further.

ARCHIMEDES INVENTED PI.

Mmm! I like pie. Was it a fruit pie, Daddy?
Ha! Not that kind of pie! Pi is a number that always stays the same.

Archimedes says...

Make some marks on a line which are exactly the width of a wheel.
1
2
3
4
0
1
2
3
4

Draw an arrow on the wheel, then point it down towards the first mark on the ground.

Roll the wheel and the arrow will go round. When it points straight down again, the distance from the start tells you how far it has travelled.

This is the same as the length of the outside of the wheel, which is called the **Circumference**. It is 3.14 times the width of the wheel. That's the number we call **Pi** or π.

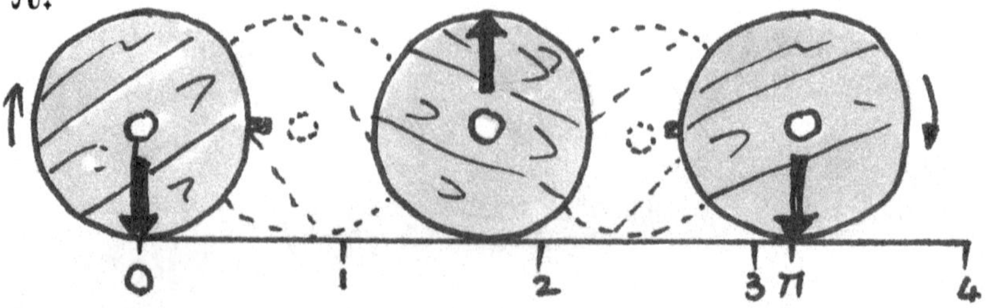
0
1
2
3 π
4

A wheel is a disk. The distance from the centre to the outside of a disc is called the ***Radius*** or ***r***. The circumference is written as $2\pi r$

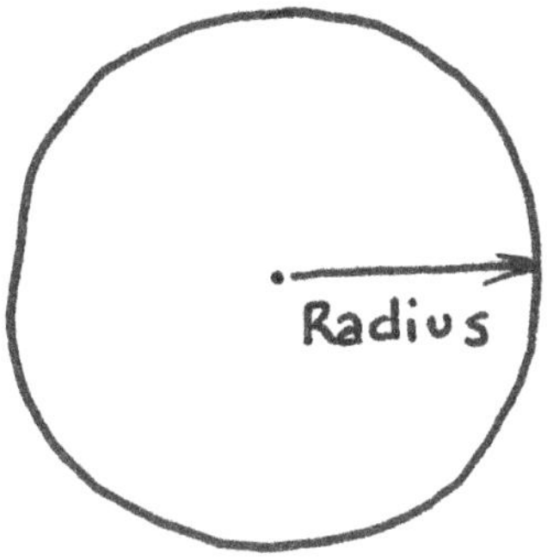
Radius

You can find the **area** of the disk by multiplying the radius by itself and then multiplying by π.
This is written as πr^2

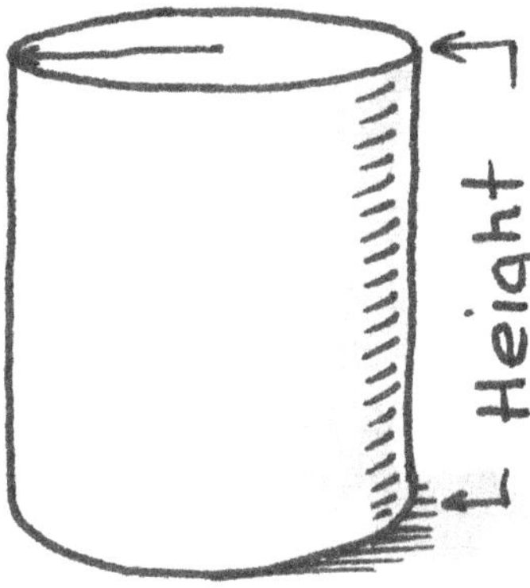
Height

The surface of a cylinder equals the circumference multiplied by the height plus the surface areas of the two disks at each end.

You can work out the surface area with the formula: $2\pi r^2+2\pi rh$

The surface area of a sphere - which is a bit like the skin of an orange - works out to be four times the area of the disk that is revealed when you cut the sphere in half, or $4\pi r^2$

You can work out the volume of the sphere too. But I'm far too busy choosing between an orange or a fruit pie to do that now!

Archimedes invented the Screw Pump

Did Pi help Archimedes invent the Death Ray, Daddy?
Ha! Ha! No! But inventing Pi made Archimedes think about circles all day long.

I see circles everywhere! But now I see spirals too. I see spirals in seeds and shells and curly hair.

One day, Archimedes picked a seashell up from the beach . When he rotated the shell, water came out of the hole at the top where it was broken.

He put the bottom of the shell under water and turned the shell again. More water came out at the top. He cut the shell open to see how it was made.

This spiral allows water
to travel upwards!

Up until then, the only way to lift water from the river, to irrigate a field, was by using one of Archimedes lever type cranes, which had a bucket at one end and a counterweight at the other, to make it easy to lift.

Archimedes Screw Pump meant that water could be raised from the river with a continuous flow by just turning a handle.

Out of simple shapes and thoughts
come great inventions.

But what about the Death Ray, Daddy? Tell me about that. It sounds so exciting!
The Death Ray was used in the Punic War, when we Romans were fighting the Carthagineans who had ruled the Island if Sicily.

"Archimedes was born in the city of Syracuse, on the island of Sicily. Most of the people of Syracuse were Greek. Their king, Hiero, was friends with Rome for a while, but then he changed his mind."

MAP OF SICILY
ROME
ITALY
Mediterranean Sea
SICILY
IONIAN SEA
SYRACUSE

"We Romans battled to win the city for two, long years. The Roman Navy surrounded the city with ships, but the people of Syracuse were clever. They had lots of food and water and the walls of the city were very strong."

"We could only attack from the sea, and Archimedes was ready for us with all his great inventions."

And Archimedes' greatest invention was the Death Ray, wasn't it Daddy?
Well, some people say that his greatest invention was his method of measuring gold.

ARCHIMEDES PRINCIPLE

I love the colour of gold!

King Hiero measured the exact weight of a lump of gold. He gave the gold to a goldsmith and asked him to make him a new crown.

Hmmm!
This crown doesn't look as golden as the gold I gave to the goldsmith.

The Goldsmith made a wonderful new crown and gave it to King Hiero.

King Hiero thought the goldsmith had mixed silver with the gold and kept some of the gold for himself.

Please weigh the crown, your Majesty. It is exactly the same weight as the gold you gave me.

When the King weighed the crown, it *was* exactly the same weight as the lump of gold that he had given to the goldsmith.

The King called for Archimedes.

There's something fishy going on here, Archimedes. Can you prove that the goldsmith has mixed silver or some other cheaper metal in with the gold?

Archimedes needed to think long and hard about the problem. How could he prove that the gold had been mixed with something else?

Archimedes ran himself a bath.

There's nothing like a nice hot bath to help you think!

The bath was full to the brim when Archimedes stepped into it. Water splashed over the sides and dripped all over the floor. Archimedes lay in the bath thinking.

Now why did it do that?

Archimedes lay in the bath thinking.

The water that spilled over must be equal to the volume of my body.
But if I was made of iron and had the same volume, I would be much heavier
And if I was made of iron but still weighed the same then I would be much smaller and have less volume.
So the crown and the lump of gold that weigh the same should be of equal volume. So...

EUREKA!

Archimedes was so pleased with his idea that he leaped out of his bath and ran down the street shouting "Eureka!" which means "I have it!"

Archimedes put the crown in a bowl of water and measured the water that spilled over. He did the same for a lump of pure gold of the same weight.

More water spilled over for the crown than the gold on it's own, proving that the goldsmith had kept some of the gold for himself.

Bad goldsmith!

ARCHIMEDES INVENTED THE CLAW

Archimedes used his knowledge of levers and counterweights to invent *The Claw!* It was a terrifying machine that could lift Roman warships right out of the sea!

The Claw is lifting the ships out of the water!

The Roman ships couldn't get close enough to the city to be able to attack. Many soldiers were drowned or injured by *The Claw*.

Archimedes' inventions gave him such a fearsome reputation that roman soldiers became scared, thinking that he must have had magical powers.

He-e-elp!
The Claw is awesome, Daddy, but what about the Death Ray?

XVIII

ARCHIMEDES INVENTED THE DEATH RAY

The work Archimedes did with Pi and circles helped him devise the dastardly, evil, Death Ray!
At last! Tell me all about it, Daddy!

Archimedes realised that the outside of a circle, or the circumference, is like millions of tiny straight lines stuck together and rolled up into a circle.

A curve is made from millions of straight lines too. So a curved mirror is like millions of little mirrors all pointing at the same spot.
The light from the curved mirror can be focussed into a pinpoint of light.
The pinpoint of light burns, as the Sun's rays are concentrated to make intense heat!

Archimedes made huge, bright, shiny, curved mirrors and placed them on the walls of Syracuse. They were designed so that the Sun's rays would be focussed at a point where the Roman Navy lay anchored.

At midday, when the sun was hottest, Archimedes' men pointed their Death Rays at the Roman ships, which burst into flames!

Wow! Archimedes was amazing, thinking up all that stuff by himself.
Archimedes was the cleverest man that ever lived, son.
So how did you win the Siege of Syracuse, Daddy? And what happened to Archimedes? Did you ever meet him?

"The citizens of Syracuse thought they were invincible and celebrated with a great feast to their goddess, Artemis, but they forgot to put guards on the walls."

"We had waited two years for such a chance. That night I gave my men special orders."

Now is the time, men.
Climb the walls and enter the city.
But do not kill Archimedes!
If we can make him work for us,
Rome will be invincible!
Hail Rome!
Hail Marcus!

XXI

"The Roman soldiers scaled the mighty walls of Syracuse, meeting little resistance as they swept through the streets, capturing the city in no time."

"Soldiers found Archimedes hard at work. But, because they were so scared of the man who invented the Death Ray, they thought his drawing instruments were magical, deadly weapons, so they killed him before he could kill them."

That is so sad, Daddy. I wish I could have met Archimedes.
Me too, son. Me too.

When Archimedes was buried, a sphere and a cylinder were carved onto his tombstone as symbols of his brilliant ideas and inventions.

ARCHIMEDES

Archimedes legacy lives on in sewage plants, grain silos, factories and farms, where Archimedes' Screw still works as well as the day he invented it, moving sludge, cereals, plastic pellets and water.

His mathematical formulae are still used every day.

Levers and cranes and pulleys are used everywhere.

The Death Ray used mirrors to focus light on a tiny spot, which gets very hot. Modern-day lasers create highly-focussed beams of light which are used to cut through metal like butter. Lasers are a modern technology, but they work on the same principals that Archimedes discovered.

Curved mirrors are used to focus light in telescopes - the same principle, but used quite differently. Gallileo, who invented the telescope was a big fan of Archimedes.

It is thought that Archimedes invented the Odometer as well. The odometer is a machine for measuring distances. Civil engineers still use a wheeled machine, that has hardly changed over time, to measure roads and building plots.

Through the many centuries that have passed since Archimedes lived, many great inventors, scientists and mathematicians have come and gone, but all of them built upon the ideas of Archimedes, possibly the cleverest man who ever lived.

If you have enjoyed this book and would like to know more about Archimedes and his inventions,
go to Shoo Rayner's website at:

www.shoorayner.com/archimedes

There you can discover more and learn how to draw circles and spheres and even draw Archimedes himself, with how-to-draw videos from Shoo's award-winning YouTube Channels.

YouTube

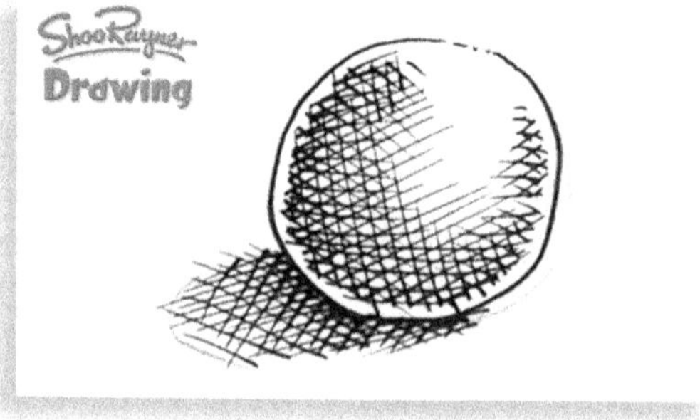
Shoo Rayner
Drawing

Shoo Rayner
Drawing
HOW TO
DRAW
ARCHIMEDES

Everyone
Can Draw
Drawing
Spheres
Part 1
Like circles in squares
Spheres fit in boxes.

EUCLID
THE MAN WHO INVENTED
GEOMETRY
Euclid
Shoo Rayner

If you love this book you may also like Euclid, The Man Who Invented Geometry.

Although Euclid lived a long time ago, his ideas are still used and taught in schools to this day.

CPSIA information can be obtained
at www.ICGtesting.com
Printed in the USA
BVHW050507110222
628611BV00003B/94

9 781908 94435